LONGBOARD SKATEBOARDING

By Peter Castellano

Please visit our website, www.garethstevens.com. For a free color catalog of all our high-quality books, call toll free 1-800-542-2595 or fax 1-877-542-2596.

Castellano, Peter.
Longboard skateboarding / by Peter Castellano.
p. cm. — (Daredevil sports)
Includes index.
ISBN 978-1-4824-2972-5 (pbk.)
ISBN 978-1-4824-2977-0 (6 pack)
ISBN 978-1-4824-2978-7 (library binding)
1. Skateboarding — Juvenile literature. I. Title.
GV859.8 C37 2016
796.22—d23

First Edition

Published in 2016 by
Gareth Stevens Publishing
111 East 14th Street, Suite 349
New York, NY 10003

Copyright © 2016 Gareth Stevens Publishing

Designer: Nicholas Domiano
Editor: Kristen Rajczak

Photo credits: Cover, pp. 1, 25 Darryl Leniuk/Stone/Getty Images; texture Standret/Shutterstock.com; p. 5 Artur Debat/Moment Mobile/Getty Images; p. 7 Jeff Gross/Getty Images Sport/Getty Images; p. 9 William Andrew/Moment/Getty Images; p. 11 Will Rodrigues/Shutterstock.com; p. 12 Trevorhall89/Wikimedia Commons; p. 13 Alan Bailey/Getty Images; p. 14 Daniel Milchev/Stone/Getty Images; p. 15 Helen H. Richardson/The Denver Post/Getty Images; p. 17 horm.ydesign/Shutterstock.com; p. 19 Christian Aslund/Lonely Planet Images/Getty Images; p. 20 Alexandro Auler/LatinContent Editorial/Getty Images; p. 21 Stanislaw Pytel/Digital Vision/Getty Images; p. 23 Ezra Shaw/Getty Images AsiaPac/Getty Images; p. 27 Forest Woodward/Vetta/Getty Images; p. 29 Darryl Leniuk/The Image Bank/Getty Images.

Printed in the United States of America

CPSIA compliance information: Batch # **CS15GS**: For further information contact Gareth Stevens, New York, New York at 1-800-542-2595.

CONTENTS

On the Board   4

All About the Gear   10

Hill Thrill   14

Skate the Way You Want   18

World Records   22

Lawbreakers?   26

Fast Fun   28

Safety Tips   30

For More Information   31

Glossary and Index   32

ON THE BOARD

Longboard skateboards have a few different uses. Many people ride a longboard to get around. But there are many daring, exciting ways to ride a longboard, too! If you've got a need for speed, longboarding could be the sport for you.

RISK FACTOR

The trick-heavy skateboarding most people know from the X Games and other **TV events** includes **vert** and street skateboarding, which don't commonly use a longboard.

All modern skateboarding started with surfers on the West Coast. They were looking for ways to practice when the waves weren't the best. The first skateboards were homemade wooden boards with roller-skate wheels attached to the bottom!

RISK FACTOR

There's a kind of surfing that's also called longboarding. The board used is 8 feet (2.4 m) long or longer, compared with the shortboard, which is only 5 to 7 feet (1.5 to 2.1 m) long.

Commercial skateboards were first sold in 1959. Boards have changed a lot since then! Different kinds of skateboarding have come about, so special boards for each kind are now made, too. However, much of all skateboarders' gear is similar.

RISK FACTOR

The first skateboarding **competition** was held in 1963 in California.

ALL ABOUT THE GEAR

Skateboards have three main parts: the deck, the **trucks**, and the wheels. The deck, or the part the skater stands on, is longer and wider on a longboard than on a trick skateboard. Some longboards also have a stiffer deck than other boards to help keep the rider in place.

RISK FACTOR

Longboard wheels are bigger and softer than those on trick skateboards. They make it easier to go fast and travel over bumpy ground.

WHEELS

DECK

TRUCK

11

Whether riding for travel or sport, all longboarders need to wear safety gear. Skateboarders fall a lot, even pros! Therefore, special helmets that fit well should always be worn. Knee and elbow pads as well as wrist guards and a mouth guard are important, too.

RISK FACTOR

As with all skateboarding, it's easy to get hurt longboarding. Learn how to fall when you first start skating, especially if you plan on riding at high speeds.

HILL THRILL

The most daring longboarders race down steep hills. This is called downhill longboarding, and it's sometimes an event in competitions. Those who race in downhill longboarding may go as fast as a car on a highway! The first one to cross the finish line wins.

RISK FACTOR

If you want to try downhill longboarding, it's safer to start with small hills on a road without a lot of cars.

One well-known place for downhill races is in Teutonia, Brazil. The track there is known as the fastest in the world. It's a special challenge for downhill racers! The Maryhill Festival of Speed is another event at which longboarders show their skills.

RISK FACTOR

Downhill skateboarding is sometimes called a "gravity sport" because movement depends on the pull of gravity.

SKATE THE WAY YOU WANT

Some skaters truly look like they're surfing on the sidewalk with their longboard. These skaters carve, or lean right and left to skate in an "S" shape, to stay in control. Skating around **obstacles**, or slaloming, makes this harder.

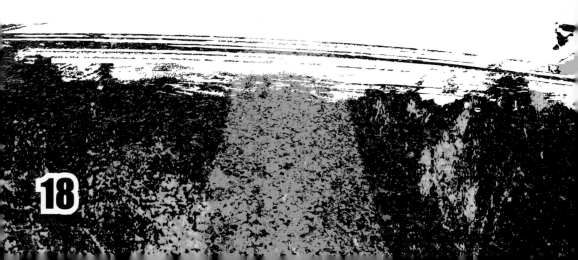

RISK FACTOR

Since the longboard can travel fast, it's a good choice for someone who wants to skateboard to get to school or work.

If you're doing some tricks on your longboard, you're freeriding! Freeriders like to ride in skatepark bowls and try **grabs**. Longboard dancing also takes a special kind of skill. The boarder walks up and down the longboard to speed up, slow down, and turn. It's tough to be good at it!

RISK FACTOR

Longboards are good for mountain boarding,
too. Skateboarders ride mountain bike courses
that can be quite steep and full of obstacles.

WORLD RECORDS

In 2012, Mischo Erban clocked the fastest longboard speed on record. He rode down a very steep hill in Québec, Canada, at 80.74 miles (129.94 km) per hour! Now that takes some daring.

RISK FACTOR

After breaking the world record, Erban said: "There isn't a single hill out there that has me scared."

Rob Thomson holds the world record for longest skateboarding journey. He rode across part of Europe, then across the United States and China. His trip added up to a total of 7,555.25 miles (12,159 km) on a longboard!

RISK FACTOR

Thomson also biked from South Korea to Switzerland.

LAWBREAKERS?

Some longboarders aren't just daredevils—they're breaking the law! Longboarding and skateboarding are illegal in some cities, except in certain areas. Sometimes, skateboarders can be fined. Police and government officials worry about the safety of skateboarders sharing the road with cars.

RISK FACTOR

In West Vancouver, British Columbia, longboarders aren't supposed to ride on the hilly city streets. Cars not seeing boarders or boarders zooming through stoplights have caused many serious car accidents.

FAST FUN

Longboarding is becoming more popular. Daredevils interested in snowboarding and trick skateboarding are some of those trying out the speedy thrill of longboard skateboarding. New ways of riding and bigger tricks are sure to follow. It's clear that there's no slowing longboarders down!

RISK FACTOR

One trick every longboarder should learn is to brake by sliding. This means turning the board so you're going sideways and sliding the wheels along the ground to stop.

SAFETY TIPS

- Wear a helmet and other safety gear every time you ride.

- Keep your board in good shape, checking for problems before using it.

- Follow traffic laws to keep out of cars' way.

- Know your skill level. Some tricks and uneven ground will be too hard for beginners.

- Stay fit in other ways to stay injury-free.

- Never ride at night or in wet or icy weather.

FOR MORE INFORMATION

BOOKS

Beal, Becky. *Skateboarding: The Ultimate Guide*. Santa Barbara, CA: ABC-CLIO, LLC, 2013.

Thomas, Isabel. *Board Sports*. Minneapolis, MN: Lerner Publications Company, 2012.

WEBSITES

How to Choose the Right Longboard Skateboard

www.the-house.com/portal/best-beginner-longboard/

Which board is right for you? Use this website to find out!

Longboarding

www.kidzworld.com/article/25390-longboarding

Find out more about how to stay safe when longboarding.

GLOSSARY

commercial: made for the public

competition: a contest someone tries to win

event: a happening

grab: a skateboarding trick in which the skateboarder grabs the side of the board while in the air

gravity: the force that pulls objects toward Earth's center

obstacle: something that blocks a path

truck: the T-shaped piece of metal that attaches a skateboard wheel to the underside of the deck

vert: short for "vertical," an event in skateboarding involving a ramp and the skateboarder changing from horizontal movement to vertical movement to do a trick

INDEX

deck 10

downhill longboarding 14, 15, 16, 17

Erban, Mischo 22, 23

freeriding 20

longboard dancing 20

mountain boarding 21

races 14, 16

safety gear 12, 30

surfing 6, 18

Thomson, Rob 24, 25

trucks 10

wheels 10